A Joy to Remember

A Joy To Remember

A Keepsake Collection of Timeless Thoughts And Familiar Sayings

Illustrated by Wendie Collins

♔ Hallmark Editions

Editorial Research: Tina Hacker
Editorial Direction: Aileene Neighbors

Acknowledgment:
1 Peter 4:8; Ecclesiastes 3:1; 1 Corinthians 13:11,13; Psalms 23:4,
33:5; Song of Solomon 2:12; Matthew 7:7; Hebrews 11:1;
Proverbs 15:13, 22:6; Mark 10:14 from the *King James Version Bible.*
Reprinted by permission of the Cambridge University Press.
Published by the Syndics of Cambridge University Press.

Come, Share the Joy

Now and then we all come upon quotations or sayings that are truly memorable — delightful expressions so rich in wisdom and meaning that we can't help thinking, "I wish I'd said that!" Some have the ring of classics, such as John Keats's immortal line, "A thing of beauty is a joy forever." Others, such as the old familiar folk maxim, "Be it ever so humble, there's no place like home," have a more down-to-earth charm. But, marvelously, all of them manage to pack centuries of common sense into a few colorful, well-chosen words.

A Joy to Remember is a unique collection of these ageless gems of insight and inspiration. Here are beautiful thoughts that warm the heart and lift the spirit — timeless words that help you gain a deeper understanding of life and cause you to smile — inside. Here, also, you will find space to jot down any new proverbs, mottos or adages that you may discover and wish to preserve for future reference.

This handsomely designed edition is a keepsake that is sure to grow more valuable with each passing year, one you will enjoy reading, adding to, and sharing with family and friends — a lasting treasury of joy to remember.

Beauty is truth, truth beauty —
    that is all Ye know on earth,
        and all ye need to know.
John Keats

I want it said of me by those who knew me
best, that I always plucked a thistle and
planted a flower where I thought a flower
would grow.   *Abraham Lincoln*

Those who bring sunshine to the lives of others cannot keep it from themselves.

Sir James Barrie

No man is an island, entire of itself; every man is a piece of the continent, a part of the main.

John Donne

Ah, but a man's reach should exceed his grasp.

Robert Browning

To see a world in a grain of sand
And a heaven in a wild flower:
Hold infinity in the palm of your hand,
And eternity in an hour.

William Blake

Nothing is more highly to be prized than the value of each day.

Johann Wolfgang von Goethe

Yesterday is already a dream, and tomorrow
is only a vision; but today, well lived, makes
every yesterday a dream of happiness, and
every tomorrow a vision of hope.

from the Sanskrit

Early to bed and early to rise
Makes a man healthy, wealthy and wise.

Benjamin Franklin

All the world's a stage,
And all the men and women merely players.

William Shakespeare

Each moment of the year has its own beauty,
a picture which was never seen before and
which shall never be seen again.

Ralph Waldo Emerson

Every cloud has a silver lining.

His bark is worse than his bite.

George Herbert

There is a true music of Nature: the song of the birds, the whisper of leaves, the ripple of waters upon a sandy shore, and the wail of wind or sea. *John Lubbock*

It's nice to be important,
              but it's more important to be nice.

When the cat's away
              The mice will play. *John Ray*

Youth is wasted on the young.

Write on your hearts that every day is the best day of the year.

Ralph Waldo Emerson

If a man does not keep pace with his companions, perhaps it is because he hears a different drummer.
Let him step to the music he hears, however measured or far away.

Henry David Thoreau

A cheerful heart and smiling face
Pour sunshine in the darkest place.

A touch of love makes all things well again.

If you have one true friend, you have more
than your share.   *Thomas Fuller*

The more the merrier; the fewer, the better
fare.   *John Palsgrave*

Nothing is so easy as to deceive one's self;
for what we wish, that we readily believe.
                                Demosthenes

This above all: to thine own self be true,
And it must follow, as the night the day,
Thou canst not then be false to any man.
                        William Shakespeare

There is a pleasure in the pathless woods,
There is a rapture on the lonely shore.

George Gordon, Lord Byron

Better to remain silent and be thought a fool
than to speak and remove all doubt.

Abraham Lincoln

Trust men and they will be true to you;
treat them greatly and they will show
themselves great.

Ralph Waldo Emerson

Good humor is one of the best articles of
dress one can wear in society.

William Makepeace Thackery

People seldom improve, when they have no
other model but themselves to copy after.

Oliver Goldsmith

My idea of an agreeable person is a person
who agrees with me.

Benjamin Disraeli

Beauty is only skin deep.

Nature is full of genius, full of the divinity,
so that not a snowflake escapes its fashioning
hand.
Henry David Thoreau

A fool and his money are soon parted.

George Buchanan

I've heard a good old proverb say
That ev'ry dog has got his day.

Edward Ward

A good laugh is sunshine in a house.

William Makepeace Thackeray

Nature has given to every time, place and season splendors of its own.

A good dinner sharpens wit, while it softens the heart. *John Doran*

The early morning hath gold in its mouth. *Benjamin Franklin*

Statistics — I can prove anything by statistics — except the truth. *George Canning*

A man is known by the company he keeps. *Elbert Hubbard*

Neither a borrower nor a lender be;
For loan oft loses both itself and friend,
And borrowing dulls the edge of husbandry. *William Shakespeare*

Grow old along with me!
 The best is yet to be.
Robert Browning

If you make money your god, it will plague
you like the devil.   *Henry Fielding*

Sweet are the uses of adversity;
Which, like the toad, ugly and venomous,
Wears yet a precious jewel in his head.
William Shakespeare

Keep company with good men,
and you'll increase their number.

Music hath charms to soothe a savage breast.
William Congreve

Happiness seems made to be shared.
Pierre Corneille

What is lovely never dies, but passes into other loveliness, stardust or sea-foam, flower or winged air.
Thomas Bailey Aldrich

And now abideth faith, hope, charity, these three; but the greatest of these is charity.
I Corinthians 13:13

A loving heart is the truest wisdom.

God did not create woman from man's head, that he should command her, nor from his feet, that she should be his slave, but rather from his side, that she should be near his heart.

A merry heart goes all the day,
A sad tires in a mile.   *William Shakespeare*

A beautiful day's a mixture of
          Work and play and joy and love.

The way of truth is like a great highway. It is not hard to find.   *Mencius*

Better be alone than in bad company.

Beauty seen is never lost.
                    John Greenleaf Whittier

He laughs best who laughs last.

The proof of the pudding is in the eating.
Henry Glapthorne

Happiness is the only good.
The place to be happy is here.
The time to be happy is now.

A little learning is a dangerous thing!
Alexander Pope

Love me, love my dog.   *John Heywood*

A stitch in time saves nine.

He's a fool that makes his doctor his heir.
Benjamin Franklin

Fools rush in where angels fear to tread.
Alexander Pope

One pound of learning requires
   ten pounds of common sense
         to apply it.

If you want anything done,
            give it to the busy man.

Cleanliness is next to godliness.

To me every hour of the light and dark is a
miracle. Every cubic inch of space is a
miracle. *Walt Whitman*

The better part of valor is discretion.
William Shakespeare

Friendships multiply joys and divide griefs.

H. G. Bohn

Handsome is as handsome does.

Oliver Goldsmith

How beautiful a day can be when kindness touches it.

George Elliston

Absence makes the heart grow fonder.

Oh, better than the minting
Of a gold-crowned king
Is the safe-kept memory
Of a lovely thing.

In many things it is not well to say, "Know thyself"; it is better to say, "Know others."

Menander

Friendship that flows from the heart cannot be frozen by adversity, as the water that flows from the spring cannot congeal in winter. *James Fenimore Cooper*

Who in his pocket hath no money,
In his mouth he must have honey.
Rowland Watkins

Suffer the little children to come unto me, and forbid them not: for of such is the kingdom of God. *Mark 10:14*

All the beautiful sentiments in the world weigh less than a single lovely action.
James Russell Lowell

Nothing is more beautiful than the loveliness of the woods before sunrise.
George Washington Carver

You can't make an omelette
without breaking eggs.

The most I can do for my friend is simply
to be his friend.   *Henry David Thoreau*

The child is father of the man.
                              William Wordsworth

Haste makes waste. *Benjamin Franklin*

The greatest happiness of life is the conviction that we are loved, loved for ourselves, or rather loved in spite of ourselves. *Victor Hugo*

What joy is better than the news of friends? *Robert Browning*

Variety is the very spice of life, that gives it all its flavor. *William Cowper*

A coquette is a woman without any heart who makes a fool of a man who hasn't got any head.

The way to a man's heart is through his stomach. *Fanny Fern*

Now faith is the substance of things hoped
for, the evidence of things not seen.

Hebrews 11:1

The last straw breaks the camel's back.

John Ray

If you can't be clever, be good.

Walk on a rainbow trail; walk on a trail of
song, and all about you will be beauty.

Navajo Song

Waste not, want not.

What a desolate place would be a world
without a flower! It would be a face
without a smile, a feast without a welcome.

Francis Balfour

Necessity
    is the mother of invention.

George Farquhar

Half a loaf is better than none.

Brevity is the soul of wit. *William Shakespeare*

Oh, give us the man who sings at his work.
Thomas Carlyle

If you have built castles in the air, your work need not be lost; there is where they should be. Now put foundations under them.
Henry David Thoreau

Train up a child in the way he should go: and when he is old, he will not depart from it.
Proverbs 22:6

Every man is a volume if you know how to read him.

William Ellery Channing

If I had but two loaves of bread, I would
sell one and buy hyacinth, for they would
feed my soul.   *The Koran*

What's one man's poison
Is another's meat or drink.

Laugh and the world laughs with you,
                    weep and you weep alone.

It is better to have loved and lost,
Than never to have loved at all.
                              Alfred, Lord Tennyson

The reward of a thing well done is to have
done it.   *Ralph Waldo Emerson*

The empty vessel makes the greatest sound.
                              William Shakespeare

An apple a day
  keeps the doctor away.

For everything you have missed you have
gained something else.   *Ralph Waldo Emerson*

Love looks not with the eyes, but with the
heart.   *William Shakespeare*

The four boxes that rule the world —
Cartridge-box, Ballot-box, Jury-box and
Band-box.

The best place to find a helping hand
is at the end of your own arm.

Charity begins at home.   *Terence*

He who falls in love with himself will have
no rivals.   *Benjamin Franklin*

I never knew an hour so drear
Love could not fill it full of cheer!

A smile is a gift you can give every day.

The fall of a leaf is a whisper to the living.

Charity shall cover the multitude of sins.

I Peter 4:8

Eat to please thyself, but dress to please others.

Benjamin Franklin

Love is the reward of love.

Johann von Schiller

Every generation laughs at the old fashions, but follows religiously the new.

Henry David Thoreau

Flowers are the beautiful hieroglyphics of nature with which she indicates how much she loves us.

Johann Wolfgang von Goethe

The earth delights to feel your bare feet.

A merry heart maketh a cheerful
countenance.   *Proverbs 15:13*

Wrinkles should merely indicate where
smiles have been.   *Mark Twain*

The quality of mercy is not strain'd:
It droppeth, as the gentle rain from heaven.
                                    William Shakespeare

That love is all there is
        is all we know of love.   *Emily Dickinson*

Thinking well is wise; planning well, wiser;
doing well wisest and best of all.

When I heard the church bells ring, I thought
I heard the voice of God.
                                    Albert Schweitzer

When I was a child, I spake as a child, I understood as a child, I thought as a child: but when I became a man, I put away childish things.

I Corinthians 13:11

The most difficult thing in life is to know yourself.   *Thales*

Thy rod and thy staff they comfort me.

Psalm 23:4

April showers
　　　do bring May flowers.

Thomas Tusser

He is happiest, be he king or peasant, who finds peace in his home.

Johann Wolfgang von Goethe

If God created shadows, it was in order to better emphasize the light.

Pope John XXIII

When friends meet, hearts warm.

That day is lost on which one has not laughed.

Though we travel the world over to find the beautiful, we must carry it with us or we find it not.

Ralph Waldo Emerson

A watched pot never boils.

Beauty is such a simple thing:
A tender bud, a bird on wing.

The heart that loves is always young.

Faint heart never won fair lady.

Henry Wadsworth Longfellow

Little pitchers have big ears.

Friendship cheers like a sunbeam; charms like a good story; inspires like a brave leader; binds like a golden chain; guides like a heavenly vision.   *Newell D. Hillis*

A picture is a poem without words.

Horace

The time of the singing of birds is come, and the voice of the turtle is heard in our land.

The Song of Solomon 2:12

There's a time to wink as well as to see.

Benjamin Franklin

Be it ever so humble
    there's no place like home.

Nothing great was ever achieved without enthusiasm.

Ralph Waldo Emerson

Life without love is like a tree
without blossom and fruit.

God's in His Heaven —
All's right with the world! *Robert Browning*

Oft a little morning rain
foretells a pleasant day.

A bachelor's life is a splendid breakfast; a tolerably flat dinner; and a most miserable supper.

No one is too small
to be able to help a friend.

Never put off till tomorrow what you can do today.

Lord Chesterfield

It seems to me we can never give up longing and wishing while we are thoroughly alive. There are certain things we feel to be beautiful and good, and we must hunger after them.

George Eliot

Get your facts first, and then you can distort 'em as you please.

Mark Twain

A wise man should have money in his head, not in his heart.

Jonathan Swift

Beauty is a light in the head.

Most people are as happy as they make up their minds to be.

Abraham Lincoln

To be beautiful and to be calm is the ideal
of nature. *Richard Jefferies*

Genius is one percent inspiration and
ninety-nine percent perspiration.
Thomas Edison

The language of friendship is not words but
meaning. *Henry David Thoreau*

Ask, and it shall be given you; seek, and ye
shall find; knock, and it shall be opened unto
you. *Matthew 7:7*

Stolen kisses are always sweetest. *Leigh Hunt*

To every thing there is a season, and a time
to every purpose under the heaven.
Ecclesiastes 3:1

All's well that ends well. *William Shakespeare*

God gave us our memories so that we might have roses in December.

Sir James Barrie

It is always darkest just before the dawn.

Behold, the fool saith, "Put not all thine eggs in the one basket" — which is but a manner of saying, "Scatter your money and your attention"; but the wise man saith, "Put all your eggs in the one basket and — *watch that basket.*"

Mark Twain

Nature is the art of God. *Alighieri Dante*

A thing of beauty is a joy forever.

John Keats

A penny saved
       is a penny earned.

Marriages are made in Heaven.
Alfred, Lord Tennyson

A tree is a nobler object than a prince in his
coronation robes. *Alexander Pope*

True happiness
Consists not in the multitude of friends,
But in their worth and choice.

Ben Jonson

A friend in need
Is a friend indeed.

How sharper than a serpent's tooth it is
To have a thankless child.

William Shakespeare

You may deceive all the people part of the
time, and part of the people all the time,
but not all the people all the time.

Abraham Lincoln

Kindness is the golden chain by which
society is bound together.

Johann Wolfgang von Goethe

Give me the splendid, silent sun with all his beams full dazzling.

Walt Whitman

Men, in general, are but great children.

Napoleon Bonaparte

An ounce of mirth is worth a pound of sorrow.

Richard Baxter

The sun does not shine for a few trees and flowers, but for the wide world's joy.

Henry Ward Beecher

Look before you leap; see before you go.

Thomas Tusser

Three may keep a secret, if two of them are dead.

Benjamin Franklin

Who can doubt that we exist only to love?
We live not a moment exempt from its
influence.   *Blaise Pascal*

The sea I found
Calm as a cradled child in dreamless slumber
bound.   *Percy Bysshe Shelley*

Cheerfulness has been called
            the bright weather of the heart.

Dost thou love life? —
    Then do not squander time,
    for that is the stuff life is made of.
                          Benjamin Franklin

What is in a name? That which we call a rose,
by any other name would smell as sweet.
                          William Shakespeare

Love will blossom anywhere
As long as someone's there to care.

A friend is the present you give yourself.
Robert Louis Stevenson

When we smile, the world seems brighter;
When we smile, our cares grow lighter.

They who love are but one step from
Heaven. *James Russell Lowell*

Love is enough. *Ella Wheeler Wilcox*

One crow does not make a winter.

Conscience doth make cowards of us all.
William Shakespeare

True love's the gift which God has given
To man alone beneath the heaven.
Sir Walter Scott

You can't teach an old dog new tricks.

The one serious conviction that a man
should have is that nothing is to be taken
too seriously. *Samuel Butler*

Big things come in small packages.

Like a great poet, nature produces the
greatest results with the simplest means.
There are simply a sun, flowers, water
and love. *Heinrich Heine*

Circumstances! — I make circumstances!
Napoleon Bonaparte

Better a diamond with a flaw than a pebble
without.   *Confucius*

Men are led by trifles.   *Napoleon Bonaparte*

Praise to Thee, my Lord,
            for all Thy creatures,
Above all Brother Sun
Who brings us the day
            and lends us his light.
                              Saint Francis of Assisi

Happy is the house that shelters a friend.
                              Ralph Waldo Emerson

Time and tide wait for no man.

The beginnings of all things are small.
                                          Cicero

Wealth is not his who has it,
But his who enjoys it.

Benjamin Franklin

Ah, how good it feels —
The hand of an old friend.

Henry Wadsworth Longfellow

Two is company, three is a crowd.

It is not enough to love those who are near
and dear to us. We must show them that we
do so.

Lord Avebury

Life is for living and hoping and caring and
sharing with people we love.

None but the brave deserves the fair.

John Dryden

The flowers are nature's jewels, with whose
wealth she decks her summer beauty.

George Croly

No bird soars too high if he soars with his
own wings.   *William Blake*

We do not see nature with our eyes, but with
our understandings and our hearts.
                              William Hazlitt

Kindness is the sunshine
                in which virtue grows.

We cannot tell the precise moment when
friendship is formed. As in filling a vessel
drop by drop, there is at last a drop which
makes it run over; so in a series of
kindnesses, there is at last one which makes
the heart run over.   *James Boswell*

I never knew a man come to greatness or
eminence who lay abed late in the morning.
                              Jonathan Swift

Courtesy costs nothing.　　　*W. G. Benham*

Welcome the coming, speed the going guest.
Alexander Pope

Intelligence and courtesy
　　not always are combined;
Often in a wooden house
　　a golden room we find.
Henry Wadsworth Longfellow

I would rather be right than be president.
Henry Clay

Help yourself, and Heaven will help you.
La Fontaine

Life is most delightful when it is on the
downward slope.　　　*Seneca*

The course of true anything never does run
smooth. *Samuel Butler*

There's only one corner of the universe you
can be certain of improving, and that's your
own self. *Aldous Huxley*

When Zeno was asked what a friend was,
he replied, "Another I."

Diogenes

Birds of a feather will gather together.

Robert Burton

The world is full of beauty when the heart is
full of love. *W. L. Smith*

No sword bites so fiercely as an evil tongue.

Sir Philip Sidney

The great man
is he who does not lose
his child's heart.

What I do and what I dream include thee, as
the wine must taste of its own grapes.
Elizabeth Barrett Browning

Ignorance is bliss.

If you would have guests merry with cheer,
Be so yourself, or so at least appear.
Benjamin Franklin

The proper study of mankind is man.
Alexander Pope

Make new friends, but keep the old;
Those are silver, these are gold.

I have always believed that good is only
beauty put into practice.
Jean Jacques Rousseau

Whoever has a heart full of love always has something to give.

Pope John XXIII

It is the nature of love
      to work in a thousand different ways.

A man's home is his castle.

Out of sight, out of mind.

The earth is full
      of the goodness of the Lord.

Psalm 33:5

My Favorite Thoughts

Favorite proverbs, cherished thoughts
And words of inspiration —
Here's a place to jot them down
For future contemplation.

*Set in Janson, a typeface
designed by Nicholas Kis about 1690.
The paper is Hallmark Ivory Vellux.
Designed by Myron McVay.*